MW00389897

We Celebrate. . .

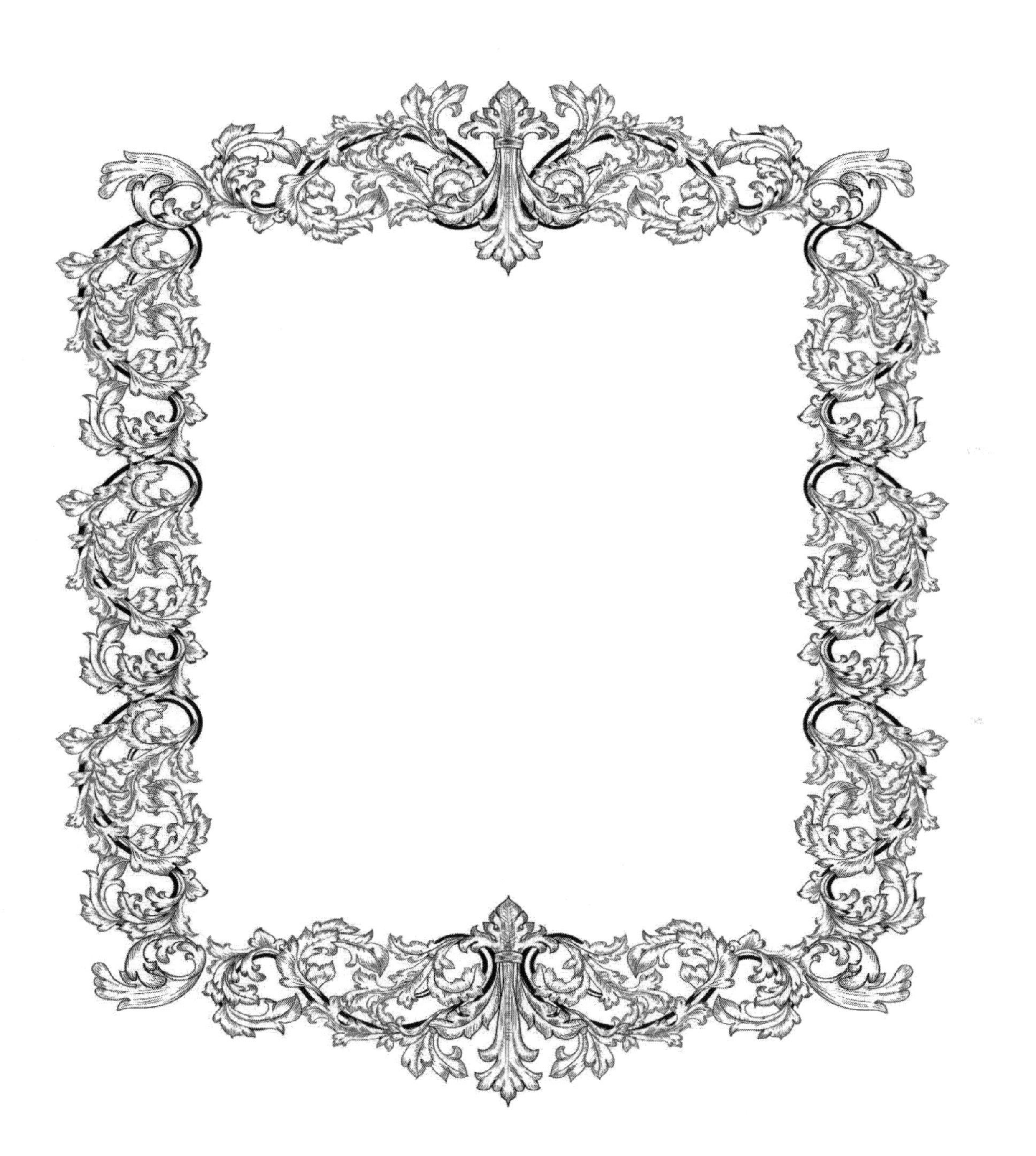

Our Family & Friends Join Us

Location

Our Celebration

Our Guests

The Party

Notes

Signatures

Letters

Great Friends

Guest Letters

Gifts Received

Guest Notes & Letters

Made in the USA
Middletown, DE
13 January 2016